Beyond the Screen

Human-Computer Interaction in the Digital Age

Writer: A. Scholtens

Cover design: A. Scholtens

© A. Scholtens

March 2023

Preface

As we increasingly rely on technology to perform various tasks in our daily lives, the importance of designing systems that are both effective and easy to use is becoming increasingly apparent. Human-Computer Interaction (HCI) is the field of study concerned with the design, evaluation and implementation of interactive computer systems for human use and with the study of important phenomena surrounding them.

Over the years, HCI has evolved into an interdisciplinary field that draws on insights and techniques from computer science, psychology, engineering, design, and other related fields. The purpose of this book is to provide a comprehensive introduction to HCI for students, practitioners, and researchers, and anyone interested in understanding the fundamental principles and concepts underlying the design and evaluation of interactive computing systems.

In this book, we will explore the different aspects of HCI, including user-centered design, interaction design, usability testing, user experience, accessibility, and the latest trends and innovations in the field. We also cover the theoretical foundations of HCI, such as cognitive psychology, human factors, and the systems approach to design.

Throughout the book we will use several examples to illustrate the concepts and techniques discussed.

Ultimately, our goal is to provide a comprehensive and practical guide to HCI that enables readers to understand and apply HCI principles and techniques to design and evaluate interactive computing systems that are effective, efficient, and enjoyable to use. Whether you are a student, practitioner or researcher in the fields of computer science, design or psychology, we hope this book will provide you with a valuable resource and inspire you to think critically and creatively about the role of technology in our lives.

A. Scholtens

Table of Contents

Chapter 1: Introduction

1.1 Definition of HCI

Human-Computer Interaction (HCI) is a field of study concerned with the design, evaluation, and implementation of interactive computing systems for human use and with the study of major phenomena surrounding them. HCI is an interdisciplinary field that draws on knowledge and techniques from computer science, psychology, sociology, anthropology, and other related fields.

HCI is a broad term that encompasses various aspects of human and computer interaction, including hardware and software design, usability, user experience, user-centered design, and evaluation of interactive systems. The goal of HCI is to create efficient, effective, and satisfying interactions between humans and computers.

HCI is an important field of study due to the growing ubiquity of computers in our lives. With the proliferation of mobile devices, wearables, and other smart technologies, our interactions with computers have become increasingly complex and varied. HCI helps to ensure that these interactions are designed to meet the needs and preferences of users, are intuitive and easy to use, and provide a positive user experience.

The evolution of HCI can be traced back to the early days of computing, when interfaces were primarily text-based and required specialized knowledge to use. As computers became more widespread and more powerful, the need for more intuitive and user-friendly interfaces became apparent. The development of graphical user interfaces (GUIs) in the 1980s was a major milestone in the evolution of HCI, as it made computing more accessible to non-expert users.

Today, HCI continues to evolve as technology advances and new interaction modalities emerge. HCI research is focused on developing new ways to interact with computers and studying the impact of these interactions on users. With the increasing importance of technology in our lives, HCI is a critical field of study that helps to ensure that technology is designed to meet the needs and preferences of users and provides a positive user experience.

1.2 The History of HCI

Human-Computer Interaction (HCI) has a rich history that dates back to the earliest days of computing. The evolution of HCI can be divided into four distinct eras, each with its own set of technological advancements and design principles.

1. The Era of Batch Processing (1940s - 1960s)

In the early days of computing, computers were large and expensive machines that were primarily used for scientific and military applications. Computing was done through batch processing, which involved submitting a large batch of punch cards to the computer, which would then process the data and return the results at a later time. The interaction between humans and computers was limited to the preparation of the punch cards and the interpretation of the output.

2. The Era of Time-Sharing Systems (1960s - 1980s)

The development of time-sharing systems in the 1960s allowed multiple users to access a single computer at the same time. This marked the beginning of interactive computing and the first attempts at developing user interfaces. Early user interfaces were text-based and required users to enter commands using a keyboard. The introduction of the mouse in the 1970s and the development of graphical user interfaces (GUIs) in the 1980s marked a major milestone in the evolution of HCI, making computing more accessible to non-expert users.

3. The Era of the World Wide Web (1990s - 2000s)

The advent of the World Wide Web in the 1990s revolutionized the way people interacted with computers. The web provided a new platform for information sharing and communication and led to the development of new interaction modalities, such as hyperlinks, web forms, and search engines. HCI research during this era focused on developing new web-based interfaces and studying the impact of the web on user behavior.

4. The Era of Mobile and Ubiquitous Computing (2000s - Present)

The proliferation of mobile devices, wearables, and other smart technologies has led to a new era in HCI. Mobile devices and ubiquitous computing have introduced new challenges and opportunities for interaction design, such as designing for small screens, touch-based interactions, and context-aware computing. HCI research during this era has focused on developing new interaction techniques and studying the impact of mobile and ubiquitous computing on user behavior.

Today, HCI continues to evolve as new technologies emerge and user needs and preferences change. HCI research is focused on developing new ways to interact with computers and studying the impact of these interactions on users. The history of HCI provides a rich context for understanding the current state of the field and the challenges and opportunities that lie ahead.

1.3 Importance of HCI in Modern Technology

Human-Computer Interaction (HCI) plays a critical role in the development and adoption of modern technology. HCI ensures that technology is designed to meet the needs and preferences of users, is intuitive and easy to use, and provides a positive user experience. The importance of HCI can be seen in several key areas:

1. Improving Usability and User Experience

HCI research focuses on understanding how people interact with technology and developing interfaces that are easy to use and provide a positive user experience. Usability testing and user-centered design are key aspects of HCI that help ensure that technology is designed to meet the needs of users. By improving usability and user experience, HCI helps to increase the adoption and use of technology, leading to greater productivity and efficiency.

2. Designing for Accessibility and Inclusivity

HCI is concerned with designing technology that is accessible to all users, regardless of their physical or cognitive abilities. This includes designing interfaces that are easy to use for people with disabilities, such as visual impairments, hearing impairments, and mobility impairments. By designing for accessibility and inclusivity, HCI helps to ensure that technology is available to all users, not just a select few.

3. Enhancing Safety and Security

HCI is concerned with designing interfaces that are safe and secure for users. This includes designing interfaces that prevent errors and accidents, as well as interfaces that protect user data and privacy. By enhancing safety and security, HCI helps to build trust in technology and promote its widespread adoption.

4. Advancing Technology and Innovation

HCI research often leads to new technologies and interaction modalities that push the boundaries of what is possible. For example, HCI research has led to the development of touchscreens, voice recognition, and gesture-based interfaces. By advancing technology and innovation, HCI helps to create new opportunities for interaction and opens up new possibilities for what technology can do.

HCI is an important field of study that plays a critical role in the development and adoption of modern technology. By improving usability and user experience, designing for accessibility and inclusivity, enhancing safety and security, and advancing technology and innovation, HCI helps to ensure that technology is designed to meet the needs and preferences of users and provides a positive user experience.

Chapter 2: Fundamentals of Human-Computer Interaction

Introduction

Human-Computer Interaction (HCI) is concerned with the design, evaluation, and implementation of interactive computer systems. To design effective interfaces, it is important to understand the characteristics of both users and computers. In this section, we will discuss the characteristics of users and computers and how they affect the design of interactive computer systems.

2.2 Characteristics of Users

2.2.1 Cognitive Abilities

Cognitive abilities refer to mental processes such as memory, attention, perception, and reasoning that are necessary for users to interact with computer systems. Users can vary widely in their cognitive abilities, which can be influenced by factors such as age, education level, and medical conditions such as dementia or ADHD.

For example, a user with poor short-term memory may struggle to recall information that is presented in a complex or convoluted way. A user with attention deficit disorder (ADD) may find it difficult to focus on a task that requires sustained attention, such as reading a lengthy passage of text. A user with visual impairments may have difficulty perceiving small or faint visual cues on an interface.

To design interfaces that are effective and easy to use, it is important to take into account the cognitive abilities of users. This can involve designing interfaces that are intuitive and straightforward, use clear and simple language, and avoid overwhelming users with too much information or too many options.

One common approach is to use visual aids such as icons, graphics, or color-coding to help users navigate and understand the interface. For users with poor memory, interfaces can include features such as reminders, pop-up notifications, or a "back" button that allows users to retrace their steps. For users with attention deficits, interfaces can be designed with clear, concise text and minimal distractions, such as animated graphics or flashing banners..

2.2.2 Physical Abilities

Physical abilities refer to the range of physical capabilities that users have, including vision, hearing, and motor skills. These abilities can vary widely depending on factors such as age, medical conditions, and disabilities. As a result, it is important to design interfaces that are accessible and usable for users with different physical abilities.

One key area of concern is visual impairments, which can affect users' ability to see text, graphics, or other visual elements on an interface. To make interfaces accessible to users with visual impairments, designers may use high-contrast colors, larger fonts, and alternative text descriptions for images. Additionally, designers may incorporate screen-reading software or other assistive technologies that allow users with visual impairments to navigate and interact with the interface.

Hearing impairments can also pose a challenge for interface design. Users with hearing impairments may not be able to hear audio cues or other auditory elements of the interface. To address this, designers may incorporate visual cues such as subtitles or closed captions to provide an alternative means of conveying information.

Motor skills, including fine motor skills and dexterity, can also be a factor in interface design. Users with motor impairments may have difficulty using a mouse or keyboard, for example. To accommodate these users, designers may incorporate alternative input methods such as voice commands or touch screens.

2.2.3 Experience and Expertise

Experience and expertise refer to the level of familiarity and skill that users have with technology. Users can range from novices who have little to no experience with technology to expert users who have extensive knowledge and skill in using technology.

Novice users may require more guidance and support when interacting with an interface. They may not be familiar with the terminology or conventions used in the interface, or may be unsure of how to complete certain tasks. To accommodate novice users, designers may incorporate step-by-step guides, tutorials, or tooltips that provide clear instructions and guidance.

Expert users, on the other hand, may prefer more advanced features and customization options. They may be familiar with the interface and its conventions, and may want to optimize their workflow or productivity by accessing advanced features or shortcuts. To accommodate expert users, designers may incorporate features such as keyboard shortcuts, customizable menus, or advanced settings that allow users to tailor the interface to their specific needs and preferences.

In addition to experience and expertise with technology, users may also have varying levels of domain-specific knowledge. For example, a medical professional may have a deeper understanding of medical terminology and procedures than a layperson. To accommodate users with domain-specific knowledge, designers may incorporate specialized terminology or features that are tailored to the needs of the target user group.

2.2.4 Motivation and Attitudes

Motivation and attitudes refer to the psychological factors that influence users' willingness to engage with technology. Users can vary in their motivation and attitudes towards technology, which can affect their adoption and use of an interface.

Users may be motivated by different factors, such as the perceived usefulness or enjoyment of the technology. For example, users may be motivated to use a productivity app if they perceive it as helpful in improving their workflow or completing tasks more efficiently. Similarly, users may be motivated to use a game or entertainment app if they find it enjoyable or entertaining.

Attitudes towards technology can also influence user engagement and adoption. Users may have positive or negative attitudes towards technology based on their previous experiences or beliefs. For example, users who have had positive experiences with a particular type of technology may have a more positive attitude towards it and be more willing to use it in the future.

Designers can take these motivational and attitudinal factors into account when designing interfaces. To encourage user engagement and adoption, designers may incorporate features that align with users' motivations and attitudes. For example, a productivity app could be designed with a user-friendly interface that makes it easy to complete tasks quickly and efficiently, while an entertainment app could be designed with engaging visuals and interactive elements that appeal to users' sense of enjoyment.

In addition to aligning with users' motivations and attitudes, designers may also consider how social and peer pressure can influence adoption and use of an interface. Users may be more likely to adopt a technology if it is widely used by their social network or peer group. To encourage adoption, designers may incorporate social features or incentives that encourage users to share or recommend the interface to others.

2.3 Characteristics of Computers

2.3.1 Processing Power

Processing power is a crucial factor in determining the capabilities of a computer. It refers to the computer's ability to handle and execute tasks, and is usually measured in terms of the computer's clock speed, number of cores, and amount of RAM.

The processing power of a computer can have a significant impact on the performance of an interface. Interfaces that require more processing power to run, such as resource-intensive applications like video editing software or 3D modeling tools, may not run smoothly on computers with lower processing power. This can result in slower performance, lag, or crashes, which can negatively impact the user experience.

To ensure that an interface runs smoothly and efficiently, designers should take into account the processing power of the target computer. This involves designing interfaces that are optimized for the capabilities of the target computer, while still providing the necessary functionality and features.

One way to optimize an interface for lower processing power computers is to minimize the amount of resources required to run the interface. This can be achieved by using efficient programming languages, minimizing the use of complex animations or graphics, and optimizing the code to reduce processing time.

Designers can also consider providing alternative versions of the interface for users with lower processing power computers. For example, a website could offer a "lite" version of their interface for users with slower internet connections or older devices.

2.3.2 Input and Output Devices

Input and output devices are crucial components of a computer that enable users to interact with the interface. These devices include keyboards, mice, touchscreens, displays, and other peripheral devices that allow users to input commands and receive feedback from the computer.

The design of interfaces should take into account the capabilities and limitations of these input and output devices to ensure that the interface is easy to use and provides a positive user experience. For example, interfaces designed for touchscreens should be optimized for finger-based input and designed with larger buttons and controls, while interfaces designed for keyboard and mouse input should use standard keyboard shortcuts and mouse gestures.

One of the challenges of designing interfaces for different input and output devices is ensuring that the interface is consistent across all devices while still taking advantage of the unique capabilities of each device. For example, an interface designed for a touchscreen should include touch-specific features such as swipe gestures, while still providing an alternative input method for users who prefer a mouse or keyboard.

Additionally, the design of interfaces should take into account the accessibility needs of users with different input and output devices. For example, users with visual impairments may rely on assistive technologies such as screen readers, while users with motor impairments may require alternative input devices such as joysticks or switches.

2.3.3 Operating System and Software

The operating system and software of a computer play a critical role in the design of interfaces. The operating system determines how the computer interacts with its hardware and how it manages software and applications, while the software provides specific functionality and features for users.

Designers must take into account the target operating system and software to ensure that the interface design is compatible and seamlessly integrates with the target computer system. For example, an interface designed for a Mac operating system may need to be optimized for Apple's Human Interface Guidelines, while an interface designed for a Windows operating system may need to follow the Windows Design Guidelines.

Additionally, the design of interfaces should take into account the functionality and features provided by the target software. For example, an interface designed for a word processing application should include features such as text formatting and spell-check, while an interface designed for a video editing application should include features such as timeline editing and special effects.

Furthermore, designers should also consider the target user group and their familiarity with the operating system and software. Novice users may require more guidance and support, while expert users may prefer more advanced features and customization options.

2.3.4 Connectivity and Networking

Connectivity and networking capabilities play a significant role in the design of interfaces for collaborative and distributed systems. Computers can vary in their connectivity and networking capabilities, such as Wi-Fi, Ethernet, Bluetooth, and cellular data, which affect the design of interfaces.

Designers must consider the target connectivity and networking capabilities to ensure that the interface is accessible and easy to use for the target user group. For example, an interface designed for a distributed team working remotely may need to provide features that enable real-time communication and collaboration, such as video conferencing and screen sharing. This requires the interface to be designed in a way that takes into account the latency and bandwidth limitations of the network connection.

Additionally, the design of interfaces for distributed systems must also consider security and privacy concerns. These concerns include protecting user data and preventing unauthorized access to the network.

Therefore, designers must ensure that the interface design follows industry-standard security protocols and provides users with adequate control over their data.

Moreover, the design of interfaces for collaborative systems must also consider the different roles and permissions of users. For example, an interface designed for a project management system may require different levels of access for different team members. Therefore, the interface design should allow for role-based access control, which allows different users to have different levels of access based on their role and responsibilities.

Understanding the characteristics of users and computers is essential for designing effective interfaces that meet the needs and preferences of users and provide a positive user experience. By taking into account the cognitive and physical abilities of users, their experience and expertise, and their motivation and attitudes towards technology, as well as the processing power, input and output devices, operating system and software, and connectivity and networking capabilities of computers, designers can create interfaces that are accessible, usable, and engaging.

2.4 The importance of usability

Usability is a fundamental aspect of human-computer interaction (HCI) and plays a crucial role in the success of any software system or application. Usability refers to the ease with which users can use and interact with a system, as well as the level of satisfaction they derive from the experience. In this chapter, we will discuss the importance of usability in HCI and how it impacts user satisfaction, productivity, and overall system performance.

First and foremost, usability is essential because it affects the user's overall experience with the system. A system that is difficult to use or does not meet the user's needs can lead to frustration, dissatisfaction, and even abandonment of the system. Conversely, a system that is easy to use and meets the user's needs can lead to increased satisfaction and adoption rates. Therefore, usability should be a primary consideration in the design and development of any system.

Secondly, usability can have a significant impact on user productivity. A system that is easy to use and navigate can help users complete tasks more quickly and efficiently. In contrast, a system that is challenging to use and requires excessive time and effort to navigate can lead to decreased productivity and lower job satisfaction. Therefore, improving usability can directly contribute to increased productivity and job satisfaction.

Thirdly, usability can impact the system's overall performance and success. A system that is difficult to use or does not meet the user's needs can result in low adoption rates, decreased user satisfaction, and negative word-of-mouth. Conversely, a system that is easy to use and meets the user's needs can lead to increased adoption rates, positive word-of-mouth, and improved overall system performance.

Finally, usability is essential for accessibility. People with disabilities or impairments rely heavily on the usability of software systems to effectively use them. Designing software with accessibility in mind ensures that people with disabilities can effectively use software systems and perform tasks, which is essential for their participation in society.

2.5 Design Principles for HCI

Effective design principles are essential for creating interfaces that are easy to use, intuitive, and efficient. These principles help designers create interfaces that are accessible to users, regardless of their cognitive abilities, physical capabilities, or technological expertise. In this chapter, we will explore some of the fundamental design principles for HCI.

1. Visibility

Visibility refers to the ability of users to see and understand the state of the system and the options available to them. This means that the interface should be designed in a way that clearly communicates the status of the system and the available options. Visibility is achieved through the use of appropriate feedback, such as status indicators and progress bars, and by making controls and menus visible and easily accessible.

2. Feedback

Feedback refers to the information that the system provides to the user in response to their actions. Feedback is essential for providing users with a sense of control and understanding of how the system works. Feedback should be immediate, clear, and relevant, so that users can easily understand the consequences of their actions. Examples of feedback include visual cues, sounds, and messages.

3. Constraints

Constraints refer to the limitations or restrictions placed on the user's actions within the system. Constraints can be physical or logical, and they help to guide the user's behavior within the system. Examples of constraints include input validation, mandatory fields, and restrictions on the number of characters that can be entered into a field. Constraints are essential for preventing errors and reducing cognitive load.

4. Consistency

Consistency refers to the use of similar design elements and interactions throughout the interface. Consistency helps to create a sense of familiarity and predictability, which can improve the user's ability to use the system efficiently. Consistency can be achieved through the use of standard controls, menu structures, and visual design elements.

5. Affordance

Affordance refers to the visual or physical cues that suggest the function of an object or control. Affordances help users to understand how to interact with the system and what actions are possible. Examples of affordances include buttons that look like they can be clicked, sliders that can be moved, and text boxes that can be edited. Affordances are essential for creating an intuitive and user-friendly interface.

6. Learnability

Learnability refers to the ease with which users can learn to use the system. A system that is easy to learn can reduce the amount of time and effort required for users to become proficient. Learnability can be improved through the use of clear and concise instructions, progressive disclosure, and context-sensitive help.

7. Flexibility

Flexibility refers to the ability of the system to adapt to the user's needs and preferences. A flexible system can accommodate a wide range of user preferences, such as font size, color schemes, and keyboard shortcuts. Flexibility can be achieved through the use of user preferences, customizable settings, and personalization options.

8. Error Prevention and Recovery

Error prevention and recovery refer to the system's ability to prevent errors from occurring and to recover from errors when they do occur. Error prevention can be achieved through the use of input validation, clear instructions, and confirmation dialogs. Error recovery can be achieved through the use of undo and redo functions, error messages, and intuitive error handling.

9. Accessibility

Accessibility refers to the ability of the system to be used by people with disabilities. Accessible interfaces are designed to be usable by people with a range of physical, cognitive, and sensory disabilities. Accessibility can be achieved through the use of assistive technologies, such as screen readers and voice recognition software, and through the use of design elements that are accessible to people with disabilities.

2.6 The Role of Psychology in HCI

Human-Computer Interaction (HCI) is a field that combines principles from computer science, design, and psychology to create technology that is easy to use and meets the needs of its users. Psychology plays a crucial role in HCI because it provides insight into how users think, behave, and interact with technology. This chapter will discuss the various ways that psychology informs and guides the design of HCI.

2.6.1 Understanding User Behavior

The first way psychology contributes to HCI is by providing a framework for understanding user behavior. Psychologists have studied human behavior for decades and have developed theories and models that describe how people perceive, process, and remember information. These models have been used to create user-centered design principles that focus on the needs and preferences of users. For example, the Fitts' Law model is used to design interfaces that are easy to use for people with different levels of motor skills. This model describes how the time to move a pointing device (e.g., mouse) to a target area depends on the distance to the target and the size of the target area.

2.6.2 Cognitive Load and Mental Models

Another important area of psychology in HCI is cognitive load and mental models. Cognitive load refers to the amount of mental effort required to use a technology, while mental models refer to the mental representations that users form about a technology. By understanding these concepts, designers can create interfaces that are intuitive and easy to use. For example, the use of icons and symbols instead of text can reduce cognitive load, as they are easier and faster to recognize and understand. Also, consistent use of visual elements (such as color and layout) across different parts of the interface can help users form mental models and reduce the cognitive load.

2.6.3 Feedback and Reward Systems

Psychology also plays a role in designing feedback and reward systems that motivate users to interact with technology. Positive feedback and rewards can encourage users to engage with a technology more frequently, while negative feedback can discourage them. Gamification is an example of using psychology to motivate users through the use of game-like features, such as points, badges, and leaderboards. By incorporating these features into the design, designers can create interfaces that are engaging and motivating for users.

2.6.4 Emotion and Aesthetics

Finally, psychology can inform the design of interfaces by considering the emotional and aesthetic aspects of technology. People often have emotional reactions to technology and are drawn to designs that they find visually appealing. By understanding the psychological factors that influence aesthetic preferences, designers can create interfaces that are visually pleasing and emotionally engaging. Additionally, designers can create interfaces that evoke positive emotions, such as happiness or relaxation, to enhance the user experience.

Chapter 3: User Interface Design

3.1 The Importance of User Interface Design

User interface (UI) design plays a critical role in the success of any interactive system. The interface serves as the primary point of contact between the user and the system, and it influences the user's experience and satisfaction. A well-designed interface can make the user feel comfortable and confident in their interactions with the system, while a poorly designed interface can cause frustration and confusion.

Good UI design is not just about aesthetics; it is about creating an interface that is usable, efficient, and effective. Usability refers to the ease with which users can perform tasks using the interface. Efficiency refers to how quickly users can perform tasks, while effectiveness refers to how accurately users can perform tasks. A good UI design should take all three factors into consideration.

Reasons why UI design is important:

1. Enhances User Experience: A good UI design can enhance the user's experience by making it more enjoyable, intuitive, and efficient. This can lead to increased user engagement, satisfaction, and loyalty.

2. Reduces Errors and Frustration: A well-designed interface can reduce errors and frustration by providing clear and concise instructions, feedback, and error messages. This can help users feel more confident and in control of their interactions with the system.

3. Increases Productivity: A good UI design can increase productivity by allowing users to perform tasks quickly and easily. This can save users time and effort, which can lead to increased productivity and efficiency.

4. Improves Accessibility: A well-designed interface can improve accessibility by accommodating users with different physical, cognitive, and sensory abilities. This can make the system more inclusive and accessible to a wider range of users.

5. Enhances Brand Image: A good UI design can enhance the brand image by creating a positive impression of the system and the organization that developed it. This can lead to increased trust and credibility, which can help attract and retain users.

To achieve good UI design, designers need to follow some basic principles. The following are some of the key design principles for HCI:

1. Consistency: Consistency is key to good UI design. Consistent design elements such as color, layout, and typography can make the interface easier to use and understand. Consistency also helps users develop mental models of the system, which can help them navigate and use it more effectively.

2. Simplicity: Simple design is often the most effective. A cluttered and complex interface can be overwhelming and confusing to users. A simple and minimalistic design can make it easier for users to understand and use the interface.

3. Feedback: Providing feedback to users is important to keep them informed of their actions and progress. Feedback can be visual, auditory, or haptic, and it can help users feel more confident and in control of their interactions with the system.

4. Flexibility: A good UI design should be flexible enough to accommodate the different needs and preferences of users. Customization options, such as font size and color themes, can make the system more accessible and user-friendly.

5. Learnability: A good UI design should be easy to learn and use. This can be achieved by providing clear and concise instructions, help documentation, and intuitive navigation.

UI design is an essential aspect of HCI that can significantly impact the user's experience and satisfaction. A good UI design should be usable, efficient, and effective, and it should take into account the needs and preferences of the target user group. Following the key design principles can help designers create interfaces that are both functional and aesthetically pleasing.

3.2 The Design Process

User interface design is a crucial aspect of human-computer interaction. It involves designing the interface that users interact with when using a computer system, application, or website. The design process involves a series of steps that are iterative in nature, allowing for continuous refinement and improvement. In this chapter, we will explore the various steps involved in the user interface design process.

3.2.1 Understanding the User and the Task

The first step in designing a user interface is to understand the users and their tasks. This involves conducting user research to understand the needs, goals, and expectations of the target users. The designer needs to identify the users' cognitive, physical, and emotional abilities and limitations to create an interface that accommodates these needs. Additionally, the designer needs to analyze the tasks that the user will perform on the system to identify the relevant functions and features that need to be included in the interface.

3.2.2 Defining the Requirements

The next step is to define the requirements of the interface. This involves developing a list of specific requirements that the interface must meet to fulfill the user's needs and expectations. These requirements are based on the user research conducted in the first step and are used as a guide for designing the interface.

3.2.3 Prototyping and Testing

Once the requirements are defined, the designer can begin creating prototypes of the interface. Prototyping involves creating mockups of the interface that simulate the user experience. These prototypes can be low-fidelity or high-fidelity, depending on the stage of the design process. Low-fidelity prototypes are quick and easy to create, while high-fidelity prototypes are more detailed and provide a more accurate representation of the final interface.

After creating the prototypes, the designer can conduct usability testing to evaluate the effectiveness of the interface. Usability testing involves observing users as they interact with the prototype and collecting feedback on their experience. This feedback is used to refine and improve the design of the interface.

3.2.4 Implementation

Once the design has been refined and tested, the final step is implementation. This involves creating the final product based on the design specifications. The implementation process may involve collaboration with developers, who will translate the design into code and integrate it into the system or application.

3.2.5 Evaluation

The final step is the evaluation of the interface. This involves assessing the usability and user satisfaction with the interface after it has been implemented. Evaluation may involve conducting surveys, interviews, or usability tests to collect feedback from users. This feedback is used to identify areas for improvement and to inform future design iterations.

3.3 Types of User Interfaces

User interface design refers to the process of creating interfaces that allow users to interact with digital devices or software applications. User interfaces (UIs) are essential components of any digital product or service, as they serve as the means of communication between the user and the system. The design of a user interface can significantly affect the user's experience and satisfaction with the product. There are various types of user interfaces, each with its strengths and weaknesses. In this chapter, we will discuss the different types of user interfaces and their characteristics.

1. Command Line Interface (CLI)

A command line interface (CLI) is a type of user interface that requires the user to type commands into a text-based interface. CLI interfaces are typically used by developers or advanced users who prefer to interact with a system through text commands rather than graphical user interfaces (GUIs). CLI interfaces are powerful and efficient, as they allow users to execute complex tasks quickly, but they can be intimidating and challenging for novice users who are not familiar with the commands.

2. Graphical User Interface (GUI)

A graphical user interface (GUI) is a type of user interface that allows users to interact with a system through graphical elements, such as buttons, icons, and menus. GUI interfaces are user-friendly and intuitive, as they enable users to interact with the system visually, without the need to type commands. GUI interfaces are widely used in modern software applications and operating systems, as they provide a user-friendly and engaging experience.

3. Web-Based User Interface (WUI)

A web-based user interface (WUI) is a type of user interface that runs on a web browser. WUI interfaces are typically used for web applications, such as online shopping websites, social media platforms, and online banking services. WUI interfaces are platform-independent, as they can be accessed from any device with a web browser and an internet connection. WUI interfaces are easy to use and maintain, but they can be slow and less responsive than native applications.

4. Natural Language Interface (NLI)

A natural language interface (NLI) is a type of user interface that allows users to interact with a system using natural language, such as spoken language or written text. NLI interfaces are becoming increasingly popular, as they enable users to interact with the system in a more natural and conversational way. NLI interfaces are still in the early stages of development and can be challenging to implement, as they require advanced natural language processing and machine learning techniques.

5. Virtual Reality Interface (VRI)

A virtual reality interface (VRI) is a type of user interface that allows users to interact with a system through a virtual environment. VRI interfaces are typically used in gaming and simulation applications, as they provide an immersive and interactive experience. VRI interfaces require specialized hardware, such as a virtual reality headset and controllers, and can be expensive and complex to develop.

6. Augmented Reality Interface (ARI)

An augmented reality interface (ARI) is a type of user interface that overlays digital information onto the real world. ARI interfaces are typically used in mobile applications, such as navigation apps and educational tools, as they provide users with real-time information and guidance. ARI interfaces require specialized hardware, such as a smartphone or tablet with an augmented reality camera and software, and can be challenging to develop.

3.4 User-centered design

User-centered design (UCD) is a design approach that puts the needs and preferences of the user at the forefront of the design process. It involves understanding the users' goals, needs, and tasks, and designing the interface around these factors to create an effective and efficient user experience. User-centered design has become increasingly important in the development of modern technology, as it allows designers and developers to create interfaces that are intuitive, usable, and engaging.

The UCD process typically involves the following steps:

1. User Research

The first step in UCD is to conduct research to gain an understanding of the users' needs, goals, and tasks. This can involve a variety of methods, including interviews, surveys, and observations.

2. Task Analysis

Once the users' needs and tasks have been identified, the next step is to analyze these tasks to understand the steps involved, the goals of the tasks, and any potential pain points or issues that users may encounter.

3. Design Ideation

After the tasks have been analyzed, the design team can begin generating ideas for how to design the interface to meet the users' needs. This can involve sketching, wireframing, or creating prototypes.

4. Prototyping

Once the design ideas have been generated, the team can begin building prototypes of the interface. Prototypes can range from low-fidelity sketches to high-fidelity interactive mockups.

5. Usability Testing

The final step in the UCD process is to conduct usability testing with real users to evaluate the effectiveness of the interface design. This can involve a variety of methods, including user observations, surveys, and interviews.

The UCD process is iterative, meaning that the design team will continue to refine and improve the interface design based on user feedback until a final product is created.

3.5 Benefits of User-centered Design

Improved User Experience

> User-centered design puts the needs and preferences of the user at the forefront of the design process, which results in interfaces that are more intuitive, usable, and engaging.

Reduced Development Costs

> By conducting user research and usability testing, the design team can identify and address potential issues early in the design process, reducing the need for costly redesigns or revisions later on.

Increased User Satisfaction

> Interfaces that are designed with the user in mind are more likely to meet their needs and expectations, resulting in increased user satisfaction and loyalty.

Competitive Advantage

Interfaces that are easy to use and provide a positive user experience can provide a competitive advantage, as users are more likely to choose products that are user-friendly and engaging.

3.6 Interface Metaphors

Interface metaphors are a crucial aspect of user interface design that help users understand and interact with digital devices and software. An interface metaphor is a representation of a real-world object or concept used to guide users through digital interactions. By using familiar objects or concepts, interface metaphors can make the user interface more intuitive, efficient, and enjoyable to use.

Metaphors have been used in user interface design since the early days of graphical user interfaces (GUIs). The first GUIs were designed with the metaphor of a desktop, complete with a file folder, trash can, and other office supplies. This metaphor made it easier for users to navigate and manipulate digital files, as they could use familiar actions such as dragging and dropping.

Today, interface metaphors continue to be an essential part of user interface design, with many new metaphors emerging. Some common interface metaphors include:

1. Desktop metaphor

As mentioned earlier, the desktop metaphor is the most classic and widespread interface metaphor. It uses familiar objects such as files, folders, and trash cans to represent digital content and actions.

2. Calendar metaphor

The calendar metaphor is used in many scheduling and productivity applications. It uses familiar concepts such as months, days, and appointments to help users schedule and manage their time.

3. Map metaphor

The map metaphor is used in many navigation and location-based applications. It uses familiar concepts such as roads, landmarks, and compasses to help users navigate and explore digital maps.

4. Book metaphor

The book metaphor is used in many e-reader applications. It uses familiar concepts such as pages, bookmarks, and tables of contents to help users navigate and read digital books.

5. Game metaphor

The game metaphor is used in many gamification and learning applications. It uses familiar concepts such as levels, points, and badges to motivate users and enhance engagement.

6. Shopping metaphor

The shopping metaphor is used in many e-commerce applications. It uses familiar concepts such as shopping carts, product pages, and checkout processes to help users purchase products online.

Interface metaphors can be very effective, but they also have their limitations. For example, if the metaphor is not well-suited to the task at hand or the target audience, it can create confusion and hinder usability. Additionally, interface metaphors can become outdated or overused, leading to a lack of innovation and creativity in user interface design.

Therefore, it is important to carefully consider the use of interface metaphors in the design process. Designers should conduct user research to determine the most appropriate metaphor for the target audience and task, and should test the usability and effectiveness of the metaphor throughout the design process.

3..7 Design patterns and guidelines

Design patterns and guidelines play a crucial role in designing effective user interfaces. They are pre-defined solutions to common design problems and provide a set of best practices for designing interfaces that are easy to use and understand. The use of design patterns and guidelines helps to improve the consistency and predictability of user interfaces, making them more intuitive and easy to learn. This chapter will explore the different types of design patterns and guidelines and how they can be used in interface design.

3.7.1 Design Patterns

Design patterns are reusable solutions to common design problems that have been proven to work in the past. They provide a set of best practices for designing user interfaces that are easy to use and understand. Design patterns can be used to solve a variety of design problems, such as navigation, input, and layout. By using design patterns, designers can save time and effort by not having to reinvent the wheel for each new project.

There are many different types of design patterns. Let's dive into some.

Navigation Patterns:

Navigation patterns provide a set of best practices for designing navigation menus and interfaces. These patterns include hierarchical, flat, and hub and spoke navigation.

Input Patterns:

Input patterns provide a set of best practices for designing input fields and controls. These patterns include form layouts, input validation, and default values.

Layout Patterns:

>Layout patterns provide a set of best practices for designing the layout of user interfaces. These patterns include grid layouts, card layouts, and tabbed interfaces.

Interaction Patterns:

>Interaction patterns provide a set of best practices for designing user interactions. These patterns include drag and drop, hover, and swipe.

Design patterns provide a common language for designers to communicate with each other. They also help to improve the consistency and predictability of user interfaces, making them more intuitive and easy to learn. By using design patterns, designers can focus on solving new and unique design problems, rather than spending time on common design problems that have already been solved.

3.7.2 Design Guidelines

Design guidelines provide a set of best practices for designing user interfaces. They are based on research and empirical evidence and provide a set of rules for designing interfaces that are easy to use and understand. Design guidelines cover a wide range of topics, including typography, color, layout, and interaction design.

Design guidelines are useful because they provide a set of rules for designing interfaces that are easy to use and understand. They help to ensure that interfaces are consistent and predictable, making them more intuitive and easy to learn. Design guidelines also help to reduce the cognitive load on users, allowing them to focus on completing tasks rather than figuring out how to use the interface.

3.7.3 Using Design Patterns and Guidelines

Design patterns and guidelines can be used together to create effective user interfaces. Designers can use design patterns to solve common design problems and design guidelines to ensure that the interface is easy to use and understand. By using both design patterns and guidelines, designers can create interfaces that are intuitive, easy to learn, and consistent.

When using design patterns and guidelines, it is important to remember that they are not a substitute for user research. While design patterns and guidelines provide a set of best practices, they do not guarantee that the interface will be easy to use for all users. User research is still necessary to identify user needs and preferences and to ensure that the interface is designed to meet those needs.

Chapter 4: Interaction Techniques and Technologies

4.1 Interaction Techniques

Interaction techniques are the methods or ways in which users can interact with a computer system. These techniques are the foundation of user experience and play a critical role in determining the success of a computer system. The design of these interaction techniques involves understanding the human abilities, limitations, and preferences, and tailoring the system accordingly.

There are several interaction techniques that designers can use when designing user interfaces. In this chapter we will discuss the most common interaction techniques.

4.1.1 Pointing

Pointing is a common interaction technique used in modern user interfaces. It involves using a pointing device, such as a mouse, touchpad, or stylus, to select or click on objects on the screen. The user moves the pointing device to a specific location on the screen, and then clicks or taps to interact with the object.

The design of pointing devices plays a significant role in the effectiveness of this interaction technique. The size, shape, and sensitivity of the device can affect the accuracy and speed of pointing. For example, a mouse with a high sensitivity may be more precise, but it may also be more difficult to control. On the other hand, a touchpad with a larger surface area may be easier to use, but it may also require more hand movements to cover the same distance.

Pointing is often combined with other interaction techniques, such as clicking, dragging, and scrolling, to provide a more versatile and intuitive user interface. For example, the user can click and drag an object to move it on the screen, or scroll up and down to navigate a long document or web page.

Pointing is also used in conjunction with other modalities, such as voice and gesture, to provide a multimodal interface that allows users to interact with the system in multiple ways. For example, a user may use a pointing device to select an object, and then use voice commands to perform an action on that object, such as zooming in or out.

4.1.2 Gestures

Gestures are an increasingly common interaction technique in modern user interfaces. They are typically used on touchscreens or other touch-sensitive devices, although they can also be used with other input devices such as mice or trackpads. Gestures involve using hand or finger movements to interact with the computer system, often mimicking physical actions that users might perform in the real world.

Some common gestures include:

Swipe: A quick movement of the finger or hand across the screen in a horizontal or vertical direction. Swiping is often used for scrolling or moving between pages or screens.

Pinch: A movement of two fingers towards or away from each other, often used to zoom in or out of a map, image, or document.

Tap: A quick, light touch on the screen or touchpad, often used to select an item or activate a button.

Double tap: Two quick taps in succession, often used to zoom in or out of an image or document.

Drag: A movement of the finger or hand while maintaining contact with the screen, often used to move objects or scroll through content.

Rotate: A circular movement of two fingers, often used to rotate an image or object on the screen.

Gestures can be a powerful way to interact with a computer system, providing an intuitive and natural way to control and manipulate content. However, it is important for designers to carefully consider the design of gestures to ensure that they are easy to learn and use for a wide range of users. In some cases, gestures may not be appropriate or may need to be supplemented with other interaction techniques to provide a complete and accessible user interface.

4.1.3 Voice recognition

Voice recognition is an interaction technique that has gained popularity in recent years, with the rise of smart assistants and virtual personal assistants. It involves using speech to interact with the computer system, rather than relying on traditional input devices such as a keyboard or mouse.

Voice recognition technology uses a combination of hardware and software to recognize and interpret spoken commands or phrases, which are then used to control the computer system. The technology typically involves the use of a microphone, which captures the user's voice, and a speech recognition engine, which analyzes the audio input to identify the words or phrases spoken by the user.

One of the advantages of voice recognition is that it provides a natural and intuitive way for users to interact with computer systems. Instead of having to learn complex commands or memorize keyboard shortcuts, users can simply speak naturally to perform tasks or input data. Voice recognition can also be a useful accessibility tool for users with physical disabilities that may make it difficult to use traditional input devices.

However, voice recognition technology also has some limitations. For example, it may struggle to accurately recognize the speech of users with accents or speech impediments, and may require training to improve accuracy. Additionally, it may not be suitable for use in noisy environments or in situations where privacy is a concern.

Despite these limitations, voice recognition has become an increasingly popular interaction technique in recent years, and is expected to continue to play an important role in the development of new and innovative user interfaces.

4.1.4 Keyboard shortcuts

Keyboard shortcuts are a popular interaction technique that involves using a combination of keys on the keyboard to execute a command or perform a specific task. Keyboard shortcuts are commonly used in software applications and operating systems, and they can help users increase their productivity and efficiency by reducing the time and effort required to perform certain tasks.

Keyboard shortcuts can be simple, such as pressing Ctrl+C to copy text, or more complex, such as pressing Ctrl+Shift+T to reopen a recently closed tab in a web browser. Some keyboard shortcuts are universal and work across different applications, while others are specific to certain applications or software.

Keyboard shortcuts can be particularly useful for users who prefer to use the keyboard instead of the mouse, or for users who have limited mobility or dexterity and may find it difficult to use a mouse. Additionally, keyboard shortcuts can be customized and personalized to suit individual user preferences and needs.

The design of keyboard shortcuts should take into account the cognitive and physical abilities of the target user group. For example, users with visual impairments may benefit from keyboard shortcuts that use high-contrast colors or large font sizes, while users with physical disabilities may benefit from keyboard shortcuts that require minimal physical effort.

4.1.5 Menu selection

Menu selection is a common interaction technique that involves presenting users with a list of options from which they can select the desired action or command. This technique is often used in graphical user interfaces (GUIs) to provide users with a clear and organized way to access different functionalities of an application.

Menus can be displayed in different ways, such as a drop-down menu, a pop-up menu, or a context menu. Drop-down menus are often used in toolbar or menu bars at the top of the screen, and they allow users to access different functionalities by selecting a category or option. Pop-up menus are often triggered by a right-click on an object or an area of the screen, and they provide users with context-specific options or actions. Context menus are similar to pop-up menus but are usually triggered by a special key or combination of keys, and they display options that are relevant to the current context.

Menu selection is a widely used interaction technique because it provides users with a visual representation of the available options and allows them to select the desired action without the need for memorization or typing. However, it is important to design menus in a way that is clear and easy to navigate, as poorly designed menus can lead to confusion and frustration for users. Some best practices for designing menus include grouping similar options together, using clear and concise labels, and avoiding too many levels of sub-menus.

4.1.6 Form filling

Form filling is an interaction technique where users enter information into fields on a form. Forms are commonly used for a variety of purposes such as registration, application submission, feedback collection, and more. Forms can be presented in a variety of formats such as web forms, paper forms, and electronic forms.

The design of forms is important in ensuring that users can easily and accurately enter information. Forms should be designed to be clear and concise, with clear labels for each field. Users should be able to quickly identify the purpose of each field and know what information is expected of them.

Designers should also consider the layout and organization of the form. Forms should be logically organized with related fields grouped together. Forms that are too long or complex may be overwhelming to users, leading to errors or abandonment.

In addition to the visual design of forms, interaction designers must also consider the input methods for form filling. For example, on a computer, users can enter information using a keyboard or mouse, while on a mobile device, users may use touch input. Designers must ensure that the form is optimized for the input method, and that the form is responsive and easy to use on different devices.

Another important aspect of form design is validation. Form validation helps to ensure that the user enters valid and accurate information. This can be achieved through a variety of methods such as requiring certain fields to be filled out, providing feedback on the input format, or using error messages to indicate incorrect inputs.

4.1.7 Direct manipulation

Direct manipulation is a type of interaction technique where users can directly interact with virtual objects or elements on a graphical user interface (GUI) using physical actions like dragging, clicking, or tapping. It was first introduced in the 1980s as a way to make computing more intuitive and user-friendly.

The concept of direct manipulation is based on the idea that users can interact with virtual objects as if they were physical objects in the real world. This means that users can manipulate and modify virtual objects in real-time and receive immediate visual feedback on the screen. This type of interaction can be particularly useful for tasks that involve manipulating images, documents, or other digital content.

One example of direct manipulation is dragging and dropping files or folders from one location to another. Users can simply click and hold an object, drag it to a new location, and release the mouse button to drop it. This interaction is intuitive because it mimics the physical action of picking up an object and moving it to a new location.

Another example of direct manipulation is using touch gestures on a touchscreen device, such as zooming in and out of an image by pinching and spreading fingers or rotating an image with a twist of the fingers. The direct manipulation of the content on the screen feels natural and intuitive to users, which makes it an effective way to interact with technology.

Direct manipulation is often used in conjunction with other interaction techniques, such as menus and toolbars, to provide a more complete and user-friendly interface. Designers of interfaces can use direct manipulation to make their interface more engaging, responsive, and easy to use, resulting in a more satisfying user experience.

4.1.8 Natural language processing

Natural language processing (NLP) is an interaction technique that involves using machine learning algorithms to analyze and understand natural language input from users. NLP systems are designed to recognize patterns in human language and use those patterns to generate appropriate responses.

NLP systems typically use a combination of machine learning algorithms, linguistic analysis, and pattern recognition techniques to process natural language input. These systems can be used for a variety of tasks, including speech recognition, language translation, sentiment analysis, and chatbot interfaces.

One of the key advantages of NLP is that it enables users to interact with computer systems using natural language input, which can be more intuitive and efficient than traditional interaction techniques. For example, instead of having to navigate a complex menu system, users can simply ask a question or make a request in plain language.

However, designing effective NLP systems can be challenging, as they must be able to accurately recognize and interpret a wide variety of natural language input. This requires sophisticated machine learning algorithms and natural language processing techniques, as well as careful attention to user feedback and testing.

The choice of interaction technique will depend on the user's abilities, preferences, and the task at hand. Some users may find it easier to use voice recognition, while others may prefer a mouse or touchpad. The task itself may also determine the most appropriate interaction technique. For example, direct manipulation may be more appropriate for tasks that involve manipulating virtual objects, while keyboard shortcuts may be more appropriate for tasks that require rapid execution of commands.

In addition to the selection of the appropriate interaction technique, the design of the interaction itself is also critical to the success of the system. Designers must ensure that the interaction is intuitive, easy to learn, and efficient to use. This involves providing appropriate feedback to users, ensuring that the interaction does not require excessive cognitive effort, and providing appropriate cues and prompts to guide the user through the interaction.

4.2 Natural user interfaces

Natural User Interfaces (NUI) are a type of interaction technique that enable users to interact with computers in a more natural and intuitive way, mimicking real-world interactions. This approach aims to reduce the gap between the digital world and the physical world, allowing users to interact with technology more easily and efficiently. This chapter will explore the concept of Natural User Interfaces, their benefits, and the technologies that enable their implementation.

4.2.1 Introduction

The term Natural User Interface (NUI) was first introduced by Microsoft in 2007. Since then, the concept has gained increasing popularity, particularly in the context of mobile devices and the Internet of Things (IoT). A Natural User Interface is designed to be intuitive and easy to use, leveraging natural human interactions such as touch, voice, and gestures.

4.2.2 Benefits of Natural User Interfaces

Natural User Interfaces offer several benefits, such as:

Intuitive and user-friendly

> NUIs are designed to be intuitive and easy to use, reducing the learning curve for new users.

More natural interaction

> NUIs enable users to interact with computers in a more natural and intuitive way, mimicking real-world interactions.

Improved accessibility

> NUIs can be more accessible for users with disabilities or limited mobility, providing new ways for them to interact with technology.

Increased engagement

> NUIs can be more engaging than traditional user interfaces, making the user experience more enjoyable and memorable.

4.2.3 Technologies that Enable Natural User Interfaces

Various technologies are used to enable Natural User Interfaces. We've already covered some of them in an earlier chapter, so we'll limit it here to naming the technology.

Touchscreens

Touchscreens are a common NUI technology, allowing users to interact with digital content using their fingers.

Voice recognition

Voice recognition technology enables users to interact with computers using natural language.

Gesture recognition

Gesture recognition technology allows users to interact with computers using hand movements, such as waving or pointing.

Facial recognition

Facial recognition technology can be used to detect emotions, allowing computers to respond to the user's emotional state.

Motion tracking

Motion tracking technology can be used to track the user's body movements, allowing them to interact with computers using physical gestures.

4.2.4 Examples of Natural User Interfaces

There are many examples of natural user interfaces in use today. In this section we limit ourselves to briefly mentioning the examples. Some examples are dealt with in more detail elsewhere in this book.

Smart speakers

> Smart speakers, such as Amazon's Alexa or Google Home, use voice recognition technology to enable users to interact with them using natural language.

Virtual reality

> Virtual reality headsets use motion tracking technology to enable users to interact with virtual environments using physical gestures.

Touchscreens

> Touchscreens are a common NUI technology used in mobile devices and kiosks, allowing users to interact with digital content using their fingers.

Augmented reality

> Augmented reality technology overlays digital content onto the user's real-world environment, allowing them to interact with it using physical gestures.

4.2.5 Challenges in Natural User Interface Design

When you see how fast technological developments sometimes go, you would sometimes forget that there are still several challenges to overcome when designing a well-functioning natural user interface. For example, NUIs often lack the tactile feedback of traditional user interfaces, making it more difficult for users to know if they have successfully completed an action. In addition, natural user interfaces are more complex to design than traditional user interfaces. It requires a deep understanding of human behavior and natural interactions. And finally there is the limitation of the state of the technology. Technical Limitations

The technologies that enable Natural User Interfaces are still evolving and make successful implementation a challenge. Simply put, we're not that far yet.

4.3 Multimodal interfaces

Multimodal interfaces are computer systems that allow users to interact with them through multiple modes, such as speech, gestures, touch, and eye gaze. Multimodal interfaces are becoming increasingly popular because they offer a more natural and intuitive way of interacting with computers. These interfaces can also improve accessibility for users with disabilities.

A multimodal interface can combine multiple input and output modalities to enable users to communicate with a computer in a more natural and intuitive way. Users can speak commands or queries to the computer, which can interpret the spoken words and respond with synthesized speech. Or users can use hand gestures to control the computer, such as waving to move the cursor or making a pinching motion to zoom in or out. Another possibility is touch. Users can interact with the computer through touch, such as tapping on icons to launch applications or dragging items to move them around. A very new, but exciting one is the eye gaze. Users can control the computer through eye movements, such as looking at an icon to select it or moving their gaze to scroll through a document.

4.3.1 Benefits of Multimodal Interfaces:

Multimodal interfaces allow users to interact with computers in a more natural and intuitive way, shortening the learning curve for new users. It offers people with a physical disability a much better accessibility, because it is no longer necessary to use a keyboard or a mouse. It seems that multimodal interfaces are less tiring because as a user you can choose an interface that you feel comfortable with. This also offers greater flexibility in the way users interact with computers, enabling them to switch between modalities as needed.

4.3.2 Challenges of Multimodal Interfaces

But the multimodal interfaces also have quite a few challenges that need to be addressed. So is the recognition accuracy still far from optimal. This is because multimodal interfaces depend on accurate recognition of input from multiple modalities. The output depends on a correct input and that is not always easy. In addition, designing and implementing multimodal interfaces can be complex. A designer must have a good understanding of the different modalities and how they can be combined. Things like this mean that developing multimodal interfaces can be quite expensive, because in addition to specialized people, multimodal interfaces require specialized hardware and software. And here privacy issues should also be carefully considered. Some modalities used in multimodal interfaces, such as eye gaze tracking, raise privacy concerns and require careful consideration of ethical issues. In the end, everything stands and falls with acceptance by the user. Multimodal interfaces may not be familiar to all users and some may find them confusing or difficult to use or users may have concerns about what kind of (personal) data is used and stored.

4.3.3 Examples of Multimodal Interfaces

Microsoft Kinect

> The Kinect sensor combines a depth sensor, RGB camera, and multi-array microphone to allow users to control their Xbox gaming console through natural gestures and voice commands.

Apple Siri

> Siri is a voice-activated personal assistant that allows users to send messages, set reminders, and perform other tasks through natural language commands.

Google Assistant

> Google Assistant is a virtual assistant that uses natural language processing to respond to voice commands and queries.

Tobii EyeX

> Tobii EyeX is an eye-tracking device that allows users to control their computer through eye movements, such as looking at an icon to select it or moving their gaze to scroll through a document.

Leap Motion

> Leap Motion is a gesture-based controller that allows users to control their computer through hand and finger movements, such as waving to move the cursor or making a pinching motion to zoom in or out.

4.4 Virtual and Augmented Reality

Virtual Reality (VR) and Augmented Reality (AR) are two emerging technologies that have gained a lot of attention in recent years. These technologies have opened up new possibilities for interaction between humans and computers, enabling users to immerse themselves in virtual worlds or interact with digital information in their physical environment.

4.4.1 Virtual Reality (VR)

Virtual Reality (VR) is a technology that enables users to experience and interact with a simulated environment that can be similar to or completely different from the real world. This is achieved through the use of special headsets, which include displays, sensors, and tracking devices that provide a sense of presence and immersion in the virtual environment.

One of the key benefits of VR is its ability to provide a fully immersive experience, allowing users to interact with virtual objects and environments in a way that feels natural and intuitive. This has applications in a wide range of fields, from gaming and entertainment to education and training, where users can be placed in realistic simulations that provide a safe and controlled learning environment.

However, VR also presents some challenges in terms of interaction design. For example, traditional user interface elements such as buttons and menus may not work as well in a fully immersive environment, as they can break the sense of immersion and require users to look away from the virtual environment. Therefore, designers must consider alternative interaction techniques, such as hand gestures, voice commands, and gaze tracking, that work within the VR environment.

4.4.2 Augmented Reality (AR)

Augmented Reality (AR) is a technology that overlays digital information on the user's view of the physical world, often through the use of a smartphone or tablet. This enables users to interact with digital information in their physical environment, such as displaying information about a restaurant when pointing the smartphone camera at it.

One of the key benefits of AR is its ability to enhance real-world experiences by adding a layer of digital information and interactivity. This has applications in a wide range of fields, from marketing and advertising to education and training, where users can access relevant information and interact with digital objects in their physical environment.

AR also presents some challenges in terms of interaction design. For example, designers must consider how to present digital information in a way that is visually appealing and does not clutter the user's view of the physical environment. They must also consider how to enable users to interact with digital objects in a way that feels natural and intuitive, such as through hand gestures or voice commands.

4.5 Conclusion Multimodal Interfaces

Multimodal interfaces are interfaces that use a combination of different input and output modalities to enable users to interact with a computer system. This can include traditional input devices such as a mouse and keyboard, as well as more advanced input techniques such as hand gestures and voice recognition.

The goal of multimodal interfaces is to provide users with a flexible and intuitive way to interact with a computer system, allowing them to choose the input and output modalities that best suit their needs and preferences.

Designers of multimodal interfaces must consider how to combine different modalities in a way that is effective and efficient for the user. For example, using voice recognition as an input modality may be useful for hands-free interaction, but it may not be suitable in a noisy environment. Therefore, designers must consider alternative input modalities, such as hand gestures or touch screens, that work well in different environments.

Additionally, designers must consider how to present output information in a way that is clear and easy to understand, regardless of the input modality used. For example, presenting information in both visual and auditory formats may be useful for users with visual impairments or hearing impairments.

Chapter 5: Evaluation Methods for HCI

Evaluation is a critical component of the human-computer interaction (HCI) design process. It involves testing the usability and effectiveness of a product or system and collecting feedback from users to identify areas for improvement. Evaluation methods help designers and developers to understand how users interact with their system and identify any problems that need to be addressed. In this chapter, we will discuss the importance of evaluation in HCI and some common evaluation methods.

5.1 Importance of Evaluation in HCI

Evaluation is important in HCI for several reasons. Firstly, it ensures that the product or system is effective in meeting user needs and accomplishing its intended goals. A poorly designed product can result in frustration, wasted time, and reduced productivity for users. Secondly, evaluation helps to identify usability problems that may be difficult to detect during the design phase. Thirdly, it helps to improve the overall user experience by identifying areas for improvement and allowing designers to make changes based on user feedback.

5.2 Evaluation Methods

There are several evaluation methods that can be used in HCI, including usability testing, heuristic evaluation, cognitive walkthroughs, and surveys. We will cover them all in this section.

5.2.1 Usability Testing

Usability testing is a critical part of the evaluation process in HCI. It involves testing a product or system with a group of representative users to identify usability problems. The primary goal of usability testing is to ensure that the product or system is easy to use, efficient, and effective for its intended users.

During the testing, users are asked to complete tasks using the product or system while being observed by a researcher. The researcher collects data on the user's performance, as well as their subjective experience, and identifies any areas for improvement. Usability testing can be conducted at various stages of the design process, from the initial prototype to the final product or system.

There are several methods of usability testing, including:

1. Lab-based testing

This involves testing the product or system in a controlled environment, such as a laboratory. The researcher observes the user and collects data on their performance and subjective experience.

2. Remote testing

This involves testing the product or system remotely, using online tools to observe and collect data on the user's performance and subjective experience.

3. Guerrilla testing

This involves testing the product or system in a real-world setting, such as a coffee shop or public space, with a group of users. This method can be useful for obtaining feedback from a diverse group of users quickly.

4. Expert review

This involves having an expert in usability or HCI review the product or system to identify potential usability problems.

Usability testing can provide valuable insights into how users interact with the product or system and identify areas for improvement. It can also help validate design decisions and ensure that the product or system meets the needs of its intended users.

However, it is essential to note that usability testing has its limitations. It may not uncover all usability problems, and the results may not be generalizable to all users. Therefore, it is important to use a variety of evaluation methods and techniques to gain a comprehensive understanding of the product or system's usability.

5.2.2 Heuristic Evaluation

Heuristic evaluation is a usability inspection method that is used to identify usability problems in a product or system. It involves evaluating the product or system against a set of predefined usability heuristics or principles, which are general guidelines for designing usable interfaces. The goal of heuristic evaluation is to identify usability problems in the early stages of development, when it is easier and less expensive to make changes.

The process of heuristic evaluation involves a group of evaluators examining the product or system and identifying any usability problems based on the heuristics. The evaluators are typically experts in usability or human-computer interaction, and they are familiar with the heuristics being used. They can be internal employees or external consultants who are brought in specifically for the evaluation.

The heuristics used in heuristic evaluation are typically derived from existing research on usability and human-computer interaction. They are general principles that have been shown to improve the usability of interfaces.

1. Visibility of system status

The system should always keep users informed about what is going on, through appropriate feedback within a reasonable amount of time.

2. Match between system and the real world

The system should speak the user's language, with words, phrases and concepts familiar to the user, rather than system-oriented terms.

3. User control and freedom

Users often make mistakes, and the system should provide a clearly marked "emergency exit" to leave the unwanted state without undue effort.

4. Consistency and standards

Users should not have to wonder whether different words, situations, or actions mean the same thing. Follow platform conventions.

5. Error prevention:

The system should be designed to prevent errors from occurring in the first place.

6. Recognition rather than recall

The system should minimize the user's memory load by making objects, actions, and options visible. The user should not have to remember information from one part of the interface to another.

7. Flexibility and efficiency of use

The system should cater to both inexperienced and experienced users, allowing them to work efficiently and effectively.

8. Aesthetic and minimalist design

The system should not contain information or controls that are irrelevant or rarely needed. Every extra unit of information in an interface competes with the relevant units of information and diminishes their relative visibility.

9. Help users recognize, diagnose, and recover from errors

Error messages should be expressed in plain language (no codes), precisely indicate the problem, and suggest a solution.

10.Help and documentation

The system should be self-explanatory, with appropriate help and documentation available to the user at any time.

The evaluators evaluate the product or system against each heuristic and identify any usability problems. They may also make suggestions for improvements. After the evaluation is complete, the results are compiled and presented to the design team, who can use the feedback to make improvements to the product or system.

5.2.3 Cognitive Walkthroughs

Cognitive walkthroughs are based on the cognitive psychology theory of problem-solving, which assumes that users use a systematic process to solve problems. The cognitive walkthrough method was developed in the 1990s by Wharton, Rieman, Lewis, and Polson as a way to evaluate user interfaces.

During a cognitive walkthrough, evaluators follow a script that describes the task in detail, including the goal, the steps involved, and any relevant information that the user may need to complete the task. Evaluators then go through each step, asking themselves a series of questions to assess the usability of the system from the user's perspective.

You should think about questions like:

1. Will the user understand what to do at this step?

2. Will the user notice the correct action to take?

3. Will the user associate the correct action with the intended effect?

4. Will the user see that the action they took was successful?

5. Will the user know what to do next?

By answering these questions, evaluators can identify potential problems that may make it difficult for users to complete the task. For example, a cognitive walkthrough may reveal that a user is likely to get lost in a complex menu structure or that the system does not provide clear feedback when a user takes an action.

One of the advantages of cognitive walkthroughs is that they are relatively easy and inexpensive to conduct. Evaluators do not need to recruit a large group of users, and the method can be completed quickly. However, cognitive walkthroughs are not without their limitations. The method is based on assumptions about how users solve problems and may not capture all of the complexities of real-world use. Additionally, the method relies heavily on the experience and expertise of the evaluators, who may not be representative of the target user population.

5.2.4 Surveys

Surveys are a commonly used evaluation method in human-computer interaction (HCI). They involve collecting feedback from users through a series of questions, which can be administered in a variety of formats including online, in-person, or through mail. Surveys are a useful tool for gathering both quantitative and qualitative data on the user's experience with the product or system.

One of the main advantages of surveys is that they can be administered to a large number of users simultaneously, making it possible to collect a significant amount of data in a relatively short period of time. Surveys can also be conducted remotely, which can be especially beneficial for products or systems with a large user base spread out over a wide geographic area.

Surveys can provide both descriptive and inferential statistics. Descriptive statistics provide a summary of the data collected from the survey, such as the average rating of a particular feature or the frequency of a particular response. Inferential statistics can be used to make broader generalizations about the user population based on the data collected from the survey. For example, inferential statistics can be used to determine whether certain user groups have significantly different experiences or opinions about a particular aspect of the product or system.

In order to be effective, surveys should be designed carefully to ensure that the questions are clear, relevant, and unbiased. Surveys should also be pilot tested with a small sample of users to identify any potential issues with the questions or the survey administration process.

One potential disadvantage of surveys is that they rely on self-report data, which may not always be accurate or reliable. Users may have difficulty accurately recalling their experiences with the product or system, or may provide responses that are influenced by factors other than their actual experience (such as social desirability bias). Additionally, surveys may not provide in-depth information on the user's experience, as the questions are often limited to a set of pre-determined options.

Despite these limitations, surveys can be a valuable tool for evaluating the user experience of a product or system. By gathering feedback from a large number of users, surveys can provide insight into the strengths and weaknesses of a product or system, and help designers identify areas for improvement.

5.2.5 Expert reviews

Expert reviews are a type of evaluation method used to identify usability problems in a product or system. Unlike usability testing, expert reviews are conducted by trained evaluators who have a deep understanding of usability principles and heuristics. Evaluators typically examine the product or system against a set of predefined usability criteria, looking for areas of improvement. Expert reviews can be conducted at any stage of the design process, allowing designers to identify and address potential issues early on. This method is often faster and less expensive than usability testing, but it does not provide the same level of insight into the user's experience. Expert reviews can be particularly useful for small design teams or when time and resources are limited.

5.2.6 Qualitative research methods

Qualitative research methods are used in HCI evaluation to gain a deeper understanding of the user experience. These methods typically involve collecting subjective feedback from users, such as through interviews or focus groups. Qualitative research can provide insights into users' attitudes, opinions, and behaviors related to a product or system, as well as their motivations and needs. The data collected through these methods is often rich and detailed, allowing designers and researchers to gain a more nuanced understanding of the user experience. Qualitative research can also help to identify patterns and trends across different user groups, leading to the development of more targeted design solutions. However, one limitation of qualitative research methods is that the data collected is often subjective and may not be representative of the broader user population. As such, it is important to use a combination of qualitative and quantitative methods to gain a comprehensive understanding of the user experience.

5.2.7 Quantitative research methods

Quantitative research methods are often used in HCI to gather data that can be analyzed statistically. This data can provide insights into user behavior, preferences, and performance. Common quantitative methods used in HCI include surveys, experiments, and analytics. Surveys involve collecting data from a large number of participants using standardized questionnaires. Experiments involve manipulating variables in a controlled environment to measure the effect on user behavior or performance. Analytics involve collecting data on user behavior from digital sources such as website logs or application usage logs. This data is then analyzed using statistical methods to gain insights into user behavior and usage patterns. The use of quantitative research methods in HCI can help researchers and designers make data-driven decisions about the design and development of interfaces and technologies.

5.3 Conclusion Evaluation Methods

Evaluation is a crucial component of the HCI design process. It helps designers and developers to identify usability problems and improve the overall user experience. There are several evaluation methods available, each with its own strengths and weaknesses. By using a combination of evaluation methods, designers and developers can gain a comprehensive understanding of how users interact with their system and identify areas for improvement.

Chapter 6: Future Directions in HCI: Emerging technologies

The field of Human-Computer Interaction (HCI) is constantly evolving, and as new technologies emerge, the possibilities for designing better user experiences expand. Emerging technologies have the potential to revolutionize how we interact with digital systems, and there are many exciting developments on the horizon.

One emerging technology that is gaining a lot of attention is virtual and augmented reality (VR/AR). These technologies provide users with an immersive experience, allowing them to interact with digital content in a more natural and intuitive way. VR is already being used for training purposes in industries such as healthcare and education, and it has the potential to be used in a variety of other contexts, such as gaming and entertainment.

Another emerging technology is the Internet of Things (IoT), which involves connecting everyday devices to the internet and allowing them to communicate with each other. This technology has the potential to transform how we interact with the world around us, enabling us to control our environments with greater ease and efficiency.

Artificial Intelligence (AI) is also an emerging technology that has the potential to significantly impact HCI. With AI, systems can learn from user interactions and adapt to their needs, providing personalized experiences and improving overall usability. AI-powered chatbots and voice assistants are already being used in a variety of applications, and as the technology advances, we can expect to see more sophisticated and intelligent systems.

Wearable technology is another area of emerging technology that is already changing how we interact with digital systems. Smartwatches, fitness trackers, and other wearable devices provide users with new ways to interact with their digital environments, such as tracking their health and fitness data or receiving notifications directly on their wrists.

Overall, emerging technologies are transforming the HCI landscape, and the possibilities for designing better user experiences are expanding rapidly. As these technologies continue to develop, HCI professionals must stay up-to-date with the latest advancements and adapt their design approaches accordingly to create engaging, intuitive, and effective user experiences.

6.1 Social and ethical issues in HCI

As technology continues to advance and become more integrated into our daily lives, social and ethical issues in human-computer interaction (HCI) have become increasingly important. HCI researchers and designers must consider the potential impact of their work on society as a whole, including issues such as privacy, security, accessibility, and digital divide.

One key area of concern in HCI is privacy. As personal information becomes more easily accessible and valuable to companies and individuals, there is a growing need to ensure that user data is collected and used in a responsible and transparent manner. This includes issues such as data ownership, data protection, and informed consent.

Security is another major concern in HCI, particularly in areas such as online banking and e-commerce. HCI researchers and designers must consider ways to improve security measures and protect users from fraud and cyber attacks.

Accessibility is also an important consideration in HCI. As technology becomes more ubiquitous, it is essential that all individuals, regardless of ability, have access to and can use technology effectively. This includes designing interfaces that are easy to use for individuals with disabilities and ensuring that technology is accessible to those in developing countries.

Finally, the digital divide is a growing concern in HCI. As technology continues to advance, there is a risk that certain populations may be left behind due to lack of access or resources. HCI researchers and designers must consider ways to bridge this gap and ensure that all individuals have access to the benefits of technology.

In addition to these specific issues, there is also a broader ethical responsibility in HCI to consider the impact of technology on society as a whole. This includes issues such as the social and environmental impact of technology, the potential for bias and discrimination in algorithms, and the responsibility of designers to create technology that serves the common good.

As the field of HCI continues to evolve, it is essential that researchers and designers consider the social and ethical implications of their work and strive to create technology that is both beneficial and responsible.

6.2 HCI in specific contexts

Human-Computer Interaction (HCI) has become an essential aspect of various fields, including healthcare, education, entertainment, and many more. In this chapter, we will explore the future directions of HCI in specific contexts.

6.2.1 Healthcare

The use of technology in healthcare has increased significantly over the years, and HCI plays a critical role in making it accessible and user-friendly. The future of HCI in healthcare involves developing innovative solutions that make it easier for patients and healthcare professionals to interact with technology. For instance, wearable devices that can monitor vital signs and transmit data to healthcare providers in real-time have become increasingly popular. The development of Virtual Reality (VR) and Augmented Reality (AR) technology has also made it possible for healthcare providers to conduct medical procedures remotely, improving accessibility and reducing the risk of exposure to infectious diseases.

6.2.2 Education

HCI in education focuses on developing user-friendly and interactive learning experiences for students. With the emergence of Artificial Intelligence (AI) and Machine Learning (ML) technology, educational platforms can now personalize learning experiences based on the student's needs and learning style. Furthermore, virtual and augmented reality technology can help to create immersive and engaging learning experiences. The future of HCI in education involves creating innovative solutions that integrate various technologies to provide more personalized and interactive learning experiences.

6.2.3 Entertainment

HCI in the entertainment industry is focused on creating immersive and engaging experiences for users. The future of HCI in entertainment involves the development of more advanced Virtual Reality (VR) and Augmented Reality (AR) technology, which will allow users to interact with virtual environments in new and exciting ways. Additionally, advances in haptic feedback technology will enable users to feel sensations such as touch, pressure, and temperature, creating a more immersive experience.

6.2.4 Other Contexts

HCI is also essential in other contexts such as transportation, finance, and communication. In transportation, HCI is used to develop interfaces that are easy to use and provide drivers with essential information such as navigation and traffic updates. In finance, HCI is focused on developing secure and user-friendly interfaces for online banking and financial transactions. In communication, HCI plays a vital role in developing interfaces that make it easy for users to communicate with each other across various platforms and devices.

HCI has a critical role to play in various contexts, and the future of HCI involves developing innovative solutions that improve user experiences and accessibility. As technology continues to evolve, it is essential to ensure that the social and ethical implications of HCI are considered to create inclusive and equitable solutions.

6.3 Human-robot interaction

Human-robot interaction (HRI) is a multidisciplinary field that focuses on understanding, designing, and evaluating the interaction between humans and robots. It involves the study of both technical and non-technical aspects, including robot design, user interface, user experience, and social, cultural, and ethical issues.

One of the main goals of HRI is to create robots that can effectively and efficiently assist humans in various domains, such as healthcare, manufacturing, and household tasks. These robots should be able to understand human needs, preferences, and emotions, and adapt to the user's behavior and environment. For example, healthcare robots can help with physical therapy, remind patients to take their medication, and monitor vital signs.

Another important aspect of HRI is the design of intuitive and natural interfaces that allow users to interact with robots in a natural and seamless way. This includes the development of multimodal interfaces that combine visual, auditory, and haptic feedback, as well as the use of natural language processing and gesture recognition.

Social and ethical issues are also important considerations in HRI. As robots become more prevalent in society, there are concerns about their impact on employment, privacy, and autonomy. For example, the use of robots in manufacturing and service industries could lead to job loss, while the collection of personal data by robots could raise privacy concerns.

In addition, there are ethical considerations surrounding the use of robots in areas such as healthcare and military operations. For example, there are debates about the use of robots in end-of-life care and the use of autonomous robots in military operations.

To address these challenges, researchers in HRI are developing frameworks and guidelines for the ethical design and use of robots. This includes the development of transparency and accountability mechanisms to ensure that robots are designed and used in a way that is safe, ethical, and beneficial to humans.

HRI is a rapidly evolving field that has the potential to transform the way humans interact with technology. By focusing on the user experience and addressing social and ethical issues, researchers in HRI can help create a future in which robots are integrated into our daily lives in a safe, beneficial, and ethical way.

6.4 Cross-cultural HCI

Cross-cultural HCI, also known as global HCI, is an interdisciplinary field that studies the interaction between people from different cultures and technology. It aims to design and develop user interfaces that are effective, efficient, and user-friendly for users from different cultural backgrounds. Cross-cultural HCI is important because different cultures have unique preferences, values, and expectations when it comes to technology.

One of the challenges in cross-cultural HCI is understanding the cultural differences that affect the use of technology. For example, some cultures prefer to communicate indirectly and may not be comfortable with confrontational or direct communication, which can affect the design of user interfaces that involve communication. Other cultures may have different expectations regarding the use of color, symbols, and icons, which can affect the design of graphical user interfaces.

To overcome these challenges, cross-cultural HCI involves using a range of research methods, including field studies, surveys, and focus groups, to gain a better understanding of the cultural differences that affect technology use. Designers may also use cultural probes, which are designed to collect information about users' daily lives and experiences, to gain insights into the cultural context in which the technology will be used.

Another important aspect of cross-cultural HCI is localization, which involves adapting user interfaces to specific cultural and linguistic contexts. This can involve translating user interfaces into different languages and adapting the design of user interfaces to local cultural norms and preferences. Localization is essential to ensure that users from different cultural backgrounds can effectively use and interact with technology.

Cross-cultural HCI is an important and growing field that aims to design user interfaces that are effective and user-friendly for users from different cultural backgrounds. As technology becomes increasingly globalized and ubiquitous, cross-cultural HCI will continue to play a critical role in ensuring that technology is accessible to all users, regardless of their cultural background.

Chapter 7: Machine learning and HCI

7.1 Introduction

Human-Computer Interaction (HCI) is the study of the interaction between humans and computers. Machine learning (ML) is a field of artificial intelligence that enables machines to learn from data without being explicitly programmed. The integration of ML in HCI has opened new possibilities for designing more intelligent and adaptive interfaces that can respond to the user's needs in real-time. In this chapter, we will explore the current state of machine learning in HCI and its future potential.

7.2 Machine Learning Techniques in HCI

Supervised Learning

> Supervised learning is a type of machine learning in which the system is trained on labeled data. In HCI, supervised learning can be used to train systems to recognize patterns and make predictions based on the user's input. For example, a system could be trained to recognize facial expressions and respond appropriately to the user's emotional state.

Unsupervised Learning

> Unsupervised learning is a type of machine learning in which the system is not provided with labeled data. In HCI, unsupervised learning can be used to discover patterns in the user's behavior

and use them to improve the user experience. For example, a system could analyze a user's browsing history and recommend relevant content based on their interests.

Reinforcement Learning

Reinforcement learning is a type of machine learning in which the system learns by trial and error. In HCI, reinforcement learning can be used to train systems to respond to user feedback and adapt to the user's needs over time. For example, a system could be trained to adjust the font size based on the user's reading habits.

7.3 Applications of Machine Learning in HCI

Personalization

Machine learning can be used to personalize the user experience by adapting the interface to the user's preferences and behavior. For example, a system could use machine learning to recommend relevant content based on the user's interests.

Speech Recognition

Machine learning can be used to improve speech recognition, making it easier for users to interact with the computer using their voice. For example, a system could be trained to recognize the user's voice and respond to voice commands.

Predictive Modeling

Machine learning can be used to predict user behavior and preferences. For example, a system could predict what the user is going to do next based on their past behavior and adjust the interface accordingly.

7.4 Challenges and Ethical Considerations

Data Privacy

Machine learning systems require large amounts of data to be trained, raising concerns about data privacy and security.

Bias and Fairness

Machine learning systems can perpetuate bias and discrimination if they are trained on biased data. It is important to ensure that machine learning systems are fair and unbiased.

Transparency

Machine learning systems can be difficult to interpret, making it challenging to understand how they work and how they make decisions. It is important to ensure that machine learning systems are transparent and understandable.

7.5 Future Directions

Hybrid Systems

The integration of machine learning and traditional HCI techniques is an area of research with great potential. Hybrid systems can combine the strengths of both approaches to create more intelligent and adaptive interfaces.

Explainable AI

The development of explainable AI is an area of research that aims to make machine learning systems more transparent and understandable. Explainable AI can help to address concerns about bias and fairness and improve trust in machine learning systems.

Human-Centered Machine Learning

Human-Centered Machine Learning (HCML) is an emerging field that focuses on designing machine learning systems with human values and needs in mind. HCML seeks to ensure that machine learning systems are ethical, transparent, and designed to serve the needs of humans.

Chapter 8: Gamification in HCI

Gamification refers to the use of game design elements in non-game contexts to enhance user engagement, motivation, and satisfaction. In the context of HCI, gamification can be applied to a wide range of systems and applications, from productivity tools to educational software to healthcare systems.

One of the main benefits of gamification in HCI is its ability to increase user motivation and engagement. By adding game elements such as points, badges, and leaderboards, users are incentivized to interact more with the system and to perform certain actions. This can lead to increased user satisfaction and a greater sense of accomplishment when using the system.

Another benefit of gamification is its potential to improve learning outcomes. By using game mechanics to teach new concepts, users can be more motivated to engage with the content and may retain the information better. This is particularly useful in educational contexts where learners may struggle with motivation or engagement.

However, there are also potential drawbacks to gamification in HCI. One concern is that users may become too focused on the game elements rather than the actual task or goal they are trying to achieve. This can lead to a decrease in overall productivity and effectiveness of the system. Additionally, gamification may not be effective for all users, particularly those who do not enjoy games or who are not motivated by external rewards.

When implementing gamification in HCI, it is important to consider the specific context and users of the system. Designers should consider what game mechanics are most appropriate for the desired outcomes and how they can be integrated seamlessly into the user interface. Additionally, it is important to evaluate the effectiveness of the gamification elements through user testing and feedback.

Gamification has the potential to enhance user engagement, motivation, and learning outcomes in a variety of HCI contexts. However, it is important to carefully consider the specific needs of users and the goals of the system before implementing gamification elements.

Chapter 9: Brain-Computer Interfaces

Brain-Computer Interfaces (BCIs) are a rapidly growing area of research in the field of Human-Computer Interaction (HCI). BCIs are devices that enable communication between the human brain and a computer, allowing users to control devices using only their thoughts. This technology has the potential to revolutionize the way we interact with computers and other digital devices, opening up new possibilities for people with disabilities and those looking to enhance their cognitive abilities.

BCIs work by detecting and interpreting signals from the brain. These signals can come from a variety of sources, including electroencephalography (EEG), magnetoencephalography (MEG), functional magnetic resonance imaging (fMRI), and others. Once these signals are detected, they are processed by a computer algorithm, which translates them into commands that can be used to control devices.

One of the most promising applications of BCIs is in the field of assistive technology. BCIs can provide a means of communication and control for individuals with disabilities such as spinal cord injuries, amyotrophic lateral sclerosis (ALS), or cerebral palsy. By using BCIs, individuals with these disabilities can control devices such as wheelchairs, prosthetic limbs, or communication devices using only their thoughts.

BCIs also have the potential to enhance cognitive abilities. For example, researchers have demonstrated that BCIs can be used to improve attention, memory, and decision-making. These findings suggest that

BCIs could be used to develop new tools for cognitive enhancement and rehabilitation.

However, there are also significant challenges associated with the development and deployment of BCIs. One major challenge is the development of algorithms that can accurately interpret the signals from the brain. These algorithms need to be both accurate and robust, able to function reliably across a range of different individuals and situations.

Another challenge is ensuring the safety and privacy of users. As BCIs become more common, it will be important to develop protocols and safeguards to prevent unauthorized access to user data and protect against malicious attacks.

In addition, ethical considerations must be taken into account when developing BCIs. For example, questions have been raised about the potential for BCIs to be used for surveillance or mind control. It will be important to ensure that BCIs are developed and used in ways that respect the autonomy and privacy of users.

Despite these challenges, the potential benefits of BCIs make them a highly promising area of research in HCI. As the technology continues to develop, it has the potential to transform the way we interact with technology and enable new possibilities for human communication and cognitive enhancement.

Chapter 10: Assistive technologies and HCI

Assistive technologies are a type of technology designed to aid individuals with disabilities in completing everyday tasks. With the increasing prevalence of technology in our daily lives, assistive technologies have become an important area of focus for HCI research.

One area of focus in assistive technology is improving accessibility for individuals with physical disabilities. For example, interfaces can be designed to work with various types of assistive technology devices, such as screen readers or voice recognition software. In addition, interfaces can be designed to accommodate different types of input devices, such as touch screens or eye-tracking devices.

Another area of focus is improving accessibility for individuals with cognitive disabilities. For example, interfaces can be designed to use simple language and clear instructions. Additionally, designers can incorporate visual cues and graphics to aid in understanding and navigation.

Assistive technologies also play a crucial role in healthcare, where they can be used to monitor and manage chronic conditions or disabilities. For example, wearable technology can be used to monitor vital signs or track physical activity, while telemedicine allows healthcare providers to remotely monitor and communicate with patients.

One challenge in designing assistive technologies is the need for customization to meet the specific needs of individual users. This requires a human-centered approach to design that involves working closely with users and their caregivers to understand their needs and preferences.

Assistive technologies are an important area of HCI research that has the potential to improve the lives of individuals with disabilities and enhance their ability to participate in everyday activities.

Chapter 11: Conclusion

In this book, we have explored the world of Human-Computer Interaction (HCI), which is the study of how people interact with technology. We have discussed the importance of user-centered design and the different methods used in HCI to design, evaluate, and improve technology to meet user needs. We have also explored various topics within HCI, such as interaction techniques, emerging technologies, social and ethical issues, and specific contexts like healthcare and education.

Overall, this book has highlighted the importance of understanding the user and their needs in technology design. User-centered design ensures that technology is accessible, usable, and enjoyable for everyone. It also emphasizes the importance of considering social and ethical implications in technology design, and the need to create inclusive and equitable technology for all.

Looking towards the future, there are many exciting directions for research and development in HCI. As technology continues to advance, we can expect to see more developments in emerging technologies such as virtual and augmented reality, brain-computer interfaces, and machine learning. We can also expect to see continued growth in the field of assistive technologies, which aim to improve the quality of life for people with disabilities.

The field of HCI plays a critical role in shaping the future of technology. By understanding the needs and behaviors of users, we can design technology that is not only functional but also enjoyable and accessible.

As we continue to push the boundaries of technology, it is essential to prioritize user-centered design and consider the social and ethical implications of our innovations. By doing so, we can create a future where technology enhances our lives and helps us achieve our full potential.

Chapter 12: References and further reading

1. "The Design of Everyday Things" by Don Norman

2. "Human-Computer Interaction: Overview, Fundamentals, and Practice" by Julie A. Jacko and Andrew Sears

3. "The Elements of User Experience" by Jesse James Garrett

4. "Designing Interfaces: Patterns for Effective Interaction Design" by Jenifer Tidwell

5. "Interaction Design: Beyond Human-Computer Interaction" by Helen Sharp, Yvonne Rogers, and Jenny Preece

6. "Emotional Design: Why We Love (or Hate) Everyday Things" by Don Norman

7. "The Cambridge Handbook of Multimedia Learning" edited by Richard E. Mayer

8. "Virtual Reality and Augmented Reality: Myths and Realities" by Mel Slater and Anthony Steed

9. "Usability Engineering" by Jakob Nielsen

10. "Designing for Interaction: Creating Smart Applications and Clever Devices" by Dan Saffer

9 7 9 8 2 0 1 0 4 3 4 6 9